# Where Are The Fish?

by Andrew J. Lepine

# Where are the Fish?

WRITTEN BY
ANDREW LEPINE

ILLUSTRATED BY
YASEMIN ARKUN

*This book is dedicated to
Vincent and Arthur Layman*

Daphne the dolphin was the star of the aquarium.
Each day she would zip,

flip, and dip for the cheering crowds and get all the fish she could eat.

One night Daphne awoke with an urge for fish.
So, she zipped, flipped, and dipped but heard no cheers.

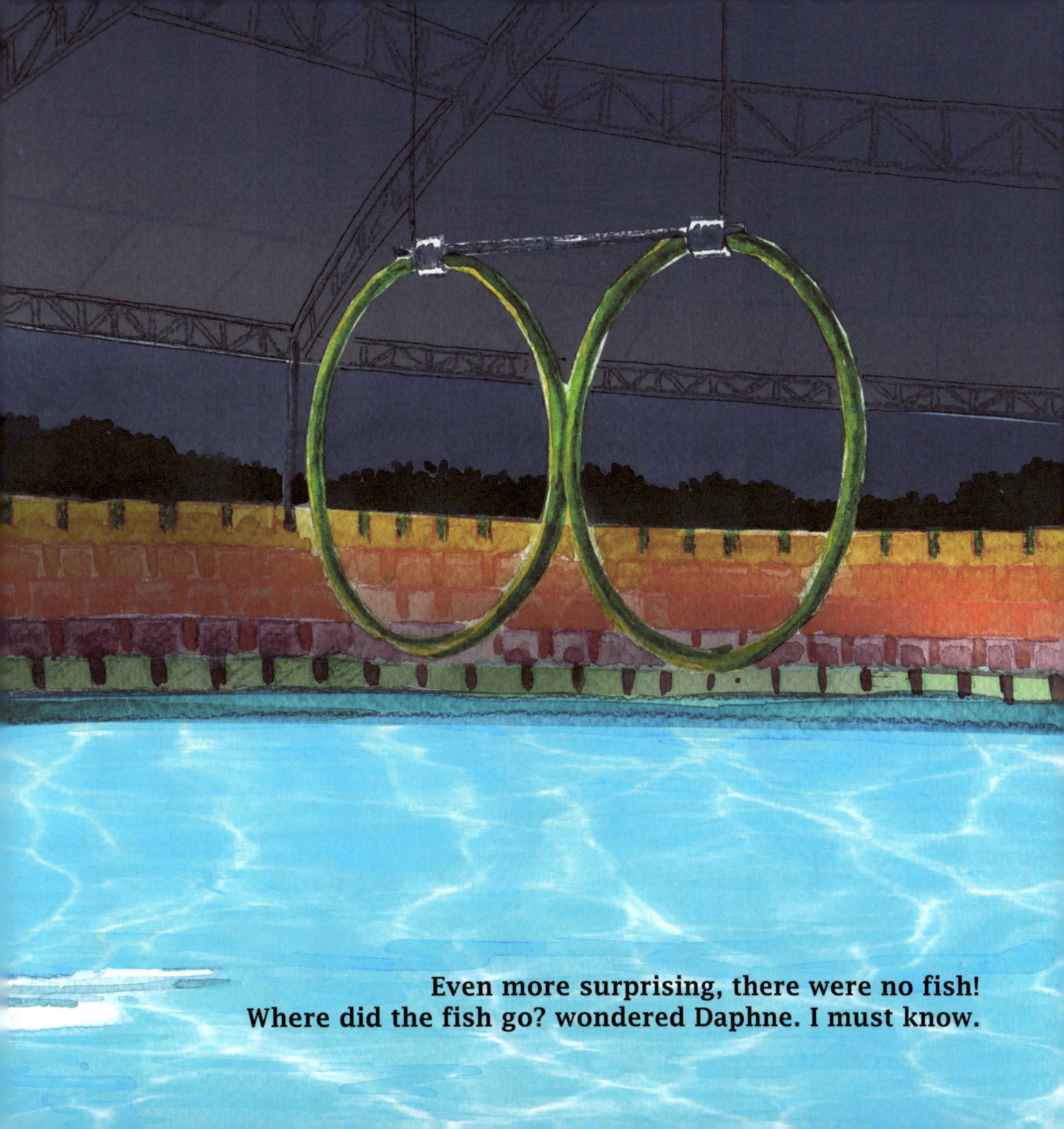

Even more surprising, there were no fish!
Where did the fish go? wondered Daphne. I must know.

She put on her hat
and jumped out of
her tank
to search for fish.

Her first stop was at the penguin pen.
"Hello, my finely dressed friends. Have you any fish?"

The penguins tobogganed into the water and whizzed through the pen.

Then all at once, they said,
"There's no fish here or anywhere,
but now we're all hungry."

"Well, come with me," said Daphne. "I'm looking for fish."

With her penguin friends in tow,
Daphne was off again until she came to the very next pen.

At first, the pen appeared empty,
but then up popped an octopus
with its eight long limbs
and three beating hearts.

"Hello, I'm Daryl."

"Hello, Daryl," everyone said.
"Have you any fish? We're hungry."

"You won't find any fish here. I've been sneaking and skulking looking for fish, but I haven't seen even one."

"Well, come with us," said Daphne. "We're looking for fish."

So, Daphne, the penguins, and Daryl
in tow went off on their way.

When they turned the corner, what did they see
but a large open tank as wide as could be.

"There must be fish in there," said Daphne,
and the group grinned.

Then, with a splish and a splash, they dove into the warm watery bath.

In the water there were wonderous things, both big and small, that the group didn't recognize at all.

"What are these all over the rocks?" Asked Daphne.

"We are the flowers of the sea, the sea anemones.
We grow in clusters and cracks, protecting
small fish from enemy attacks."

"What are these glowing things we see?" questioned the penguins.

"We are jellyfish. With our boneless bodies, we blob through the sea. With our tentacles down, we rise and we fall, not seeing because we have no eyes at all."

"Now here is a most peculiar fellow." Said Daryl.

"I am a seahorse.
I can match any color to
hide in a hurry. With my
small dorsal fin, I cannot
really scurry. I am silent and
stealthy,
feeding a lot because of the
belly I have not got."

"This is all fine and neat, but we are all looking for fish we can eat."

Then along came a sea turtle with flippers for feet, and everyone listened because it was the wise of the deep. "If you're looking for fish, then you're in for a treat.

Just down the hall is a room you should seek.
I've seen a human with buckets really deep,
piled high with all the fish you could eat."

With a thank-you and a wave,
the group took their leave and raced down the hall.
They opened the door and saw such a feast:
a mountain of fish that they all could eat.

They feasted and fed till they were all content,
before returning to their tanks and going to bed.

www.ingramcontent.com/pod-product-compliance
Lightning Source LLC
LaVergne TN
LVHW072131070426
835513LV00002B/66